Catastrophic Chords
MARCK L. BEGGS

salmonpoetry

Published in 2008 by
Salmon Poetry,
Cliffs of Moher, County Clare, Ireland
Website: www.salmonpoetry.com
Email: info@salmonpoetry.com

Copyright © Marck L. Beggs 2008
www.marckbeggs.com

ISBN 978-1-903392-89-8

All rights reserved. No part of this publication may be reproduced or transmitted in any form or by any means, electronic or mechanical, including photography, recording, or any information storage or retrieval system, without permission in writing from the publisher. The book is sold subject to the condition that it shall not, by way of trade or otherwise, be lent, resold or otherwise circulated without the publisher's prior consent in any form of binding or cover other than that in which it is published and without a similar condition, including this condition, being imposed on the subsequent purchaser.

Cover photograph: "Procol Harum 2" by Guy Webster (www.guywebster.com)
Inside photographs: Unabomber cabin photos by Richard Barnes.
                    (www.richardbarnes.net)
Cover design: Siobhán Hutson
Typesetting: Patrick Chapman

Acknowledgments

"Asparagus" was originally published in the *Oxford American* (2005). "Canadian Sonnet" was included in the anthology: *Salmon—A Journey in Poetry* (2007). "Landscape" was originally published in the *Arkansas Review* (2004). "Rautavaara," "The Poet Falls For a Pianist," and "Seven Dreams of Thoreau & the Unabomber" were originally published in *ROKOVOKO* (2007-08). Thanks to the Bloomsburywest Writers' Retreat in Silver Cliff, Colorado for peace, quiet and scenery to work on these poems.

Also by Marck L. Beggs

Books
Libido Café (2004)
Godworm (1995)

CD
dog gods: *I am large; I contain multitudes.* (2008)

Contents

I. A Finer Air

Canadian Sonnet	13
Still Life With Piano & Train	14
The Poet Falls For a Pianist	15
Grey Matters	16
Waking to Brahms	17
Brahms In the Airport	18
Rautavaara	19
Pumpkin Seeds	20
Asparagus	21
Driving Home: Sunday a.m.	22
Ode To a T-Shirt	23
The World Without You	24
Landscape	25
The Door	26
A Brief History of My Heart	27

II. A Cabin in the Woods

a. Nine Dialogues   35
    i. Prologues   36
    ii. Youth   38
    iii. Harvard   40
    iv. Teaching & Violence   42
    v. Love   44
    vi. Cabins   46
    vii. Prison/Jail   48
    viii. The Art of Writing   50
    ix. Found Poems   52

b. Seven Dreams of Thoreau & the Unabomber   55

I.

A Finer Air

I understood this when I was in Rome for the first time and saw the Moses of Michelangelo. I saw the statue as a symbol of European culture, built from two cultures in complete contrast. One source is Greek philosophy: very rational, very clear. The other is the monotheism of the hallucinating Hebraic prophets. Writing 'Vigilia,' I asked myself: how can I write hours of music so people don't die of boredom? Pärt would probably ask the opposite: how do I make the music last forever?

—Einojuhani Rautavaara

Canadian Sonnet

Now she has flown north to the white blanket
of her youth, the fields spread out like a quilt
over a past archived in permafrost:
the story of a girl, the sudden tilt

from a bench as her lungs shut out the air
and collapsed like broken wings in her chest.
Not even the chords from her repertoire
could fasten her hands, folding in like nests.

Yet you breathe still today. The noisy geese
from your homeland land in my pond, their wings
jubilant as they crash into water,
in time to fleece corn from mallards, to sing

vulgar arias in honks of cold air.
Would that one were you flown home to my care.

Still Life with Piano & Train

The yawning vowel
of a train whistle
drifted to her window
in the middle of the night.
He leaned hard toward the glass,
waiting for the note
to fall off like the sonance
she had played earlier against
the tick of a metronome.
Between each plink,
a broad silence: the whoosh
of a screen door, a step
into darkness. Like the train
slipping off beyond hearing.
Turning back into the staccato
breathing of her sleep, he wondered
where she went so deeply
to miss that sudden music.

The Poet Falls for a Pianist

She's smart in a Spartan
sort of way: sweeps her wooden floors
barren to keep the poet
from chasing dust bunnies
or following a trail of crumbs
to her bed. Keeps the poet
swooning in wonderous despair.

Her hands flex like hawkwings
over the keyboard, fingers precise
as crystals in a Swiss watch.
When she plays, he sees notes
spread out in the wind, populating
the room with her temporal children,

a wandering tribe
of tonal kin immigrating
to the desert of his consciousness.
Once settled, they call for others
and insist that he feed them all.

So the poet stands at her counter
slicing cucumbers, rinsing black olives,
and steaming thick coins of zucchini
to press like holy wafers between her lips.

Her appetite is a marvel of architecture:
the streamlined cathedral brimming
with light and soul lifting

to the bleb of her eye. Her kiss
reveals the passion of hands,

of breath pulsing her fingers to music.

Grey Matters

> *The Brain—is wider than the Sky—*
> *—Emily*

All the new thinking is about distance
And paradox: the thick blue rim of the sky,
Or the far light edge of the universe.
We are blinded by our own ambitions.

When I imagine what you must play for—
A note so perfect, music cascading
From the tips of your fingers—I hold still
And let the world pour into my mind.

All the old thinking was about love,
The distance and paradox of the heart.
We think we know better, our modern brains
Setting our sad, antiquated hearts straight.

We live like untouched keys in a rhapsody:
Aching to vibrate, to sing.

Waking to Brahms

I don't know how to talk about these things:
waking to Brahms, to the thought of your tears
as you handed him to me like a ring
slipped from your finger, music old and dear.

Nothing in my life prepared me for this:
a woman slowly setting down her fork—
a piano rumbles as a horn lifts
note after note out of dull space, forward

along a strain of violin, twisting
into each other, a vineyard of pulse—
her fingers touch the clear air, insisting
upon movement, upon silent convulse.

Head nodded, eyes closed, you manage to see
a world slipping my grasp. Talk to me.

Brahms in the Airport

In a world of white noise, universal
hideousness pervades. The very air
reeks of anxiety and monotones
yapping into cellphones. If hell can smell

worse than an elevator, or sound cheap
as country music, we have so arrived.
Then, as your teacher softly presses down
on the opening keys, and salvation

works its way through earphones, Brahms,
it would seem, was oblivious to hell. His Clara
hovering always near his heart, luring
his fingers awake, he spoke as a man

for whom love was bread. For whom life itself
brought only more music, a finer air.

Rautavaara

If birds cannot play in the concerto,
bring the music up into the air.

*If an artist is not a Modernist
when he is young, he has no heart.*

If one harp will not rise above the din,
compose for two harps to speak as one.

*If he is a Modernist when he is old,
he has no brain.*

If the poet cannot find his muse,
he needs to find his eyes.

If the pianist cannot feel the chord
within the reach of her fingers

she must play with the whole of her arm,
for the chord must be catastrophic.

Pumpkin Seeds

She is an absent-minded version
Of Gretel planting
A trail of white seeds,
Turning my cabin into a maze.

Or she is the genius sleuth
Unlocking the mystery
Of Brahms' 3rd Sonata,
Splicing notes into reels of music.

If hands could represent souls,
Hers would be prophets
Wandering the stark, ivory landscape
Calling us back into the fold.

Follow scattered seeds back to her hands;
Follow her hands to Elysium.

Asparagus

In *Love in the Time of Cholera*,
an old man's only pleasure,
left to the wilds of his faded senses,
came from the asparagus-laced scent
lifting from a stream of urine spattering
a mango tree, as he closed his eyes
and groaned. The triggers of memory
are never where we try to hide them,
but in blots of dross
dripping down the crust of bark.

Yesterday, I thought of you and worked
my fingers into a plot of soil, grinding
dark Arkansas clay into a sandy bed
where bushy crowns might flourish,
where this dirt-poor cousin of the lily
might find its way into grace.

On the day I tell you, I will steam
green stalks to the edge of crisp,
to crunch lightly beneath
your molars, between kisses
slippery with olive oil and later,
among the solitude of your waste,
you will remember.

Driving Home: Sunday a.m.

Portuguese fishermen have a word
for this exact moment, nigrescent as the spleen
of a cave: *madrugada*. Bursting through
massed fog, the air takes on the shapes
of a world morphing into existence,
and my lone headlight is barely a match
to lead me along this road, hurtling into hollow.

Leaving you is a constant fall,
the inner-eye pouring over a flicker
of tongue, a prick of cold air,
the small collapse of your body
weighing in on me. If the mind
plays tricks, how are we to know
which way the mirror reflects?

I know only this much: when you reveal
yourself to me, I know who I am.

Ode to a T-Shirt

The frayed neckline
crept up from your clavicles
where the ocean scent
of your pores opened
into my mouth, where
I inhaled the life of you.

The cracked and faded letters
of your *alma mater* sloped
down your breasts
like a spring snowscape melting
away from dark, wet branches.

In my transgression, I washed
that which held your skin,
returning it to a sterile,
inanimate condition, mere cloth.

I want to pull it on to your body,
Let it return to you.

The World Without You

is a shell held to my ear:
whispers of the sea,
the ghost of your voice
churning under waves of silence.

There was a time I craved such absence,
when the world was a harsh
slant of light against my temples.

now it has filled with the taste
of your skin, the soft taper of your eyes.

Landscape

Today the world is half exposed.
Mud and leaves soak up
a sifting of snow, a mass of scar tissue
gazing out from a torn white dress.

We know how it will all change.
Green sprigs will cast long shadows
to hide brown, a lover's tongue
tracing scars like an artist's apprentice.

Or, perhaps, this is all wrong.
The snow could turn over night
into killing frost, the scars
pulsating beneath the lover's pale skin.

Yet it is the same with the earth
as with the heart, there to be claimed.

The Door

1

Under the wide, glimmering sky
Skeining out in a lake's slow ripples,
The moon is a hollow door
Skinned by my own knuckles.

If you answered, I might survive this.

The moon is a let vein over the land,
Your eyes a draft of battle weary tears
Framing your answer, your words
Pushing me out the door.

Out here where survival is a dimming light.

Where the bleached slender bones of your past
Collapse like lungs grown apart from the valves
Of your heart, the very one from which you offered
Just enough to taste, to swallow.

A door into the wilderness of you.

2

The door to hell is not so wide
As a pair of thin lips refusing to pronounce "love."
The trap door of the brain opens
To wild speculation: who else hears
That wild moan beyond yourself?

When you shut a door, you refuse light.
Without light, we become no one.

A Brief History of My Heart

It was first discovered in a muddy shoebox
by a girl named Patsy in a field of wild poppies
in Northern California. Patsy, and her friend Lulu,
strolled hand in hand along Cattail Creek,
crossing the field to pick me up
on the way to school. That's when
Patsy tripped over the box, and my heart
spilled out, staining her shoes. According
to Lulu, she screamed in delight.

They carried it all the way to me that morning,
tossing it back and forth like a slippery ball.
I was very happy to have it back, especially
since I had been utterly unaware of its existence.
The next day, however, Patsy and Lulu
discovered some bad mushrooms
and were whisked off to the hospital
to get their stomachs pumped.
They never crossed that field again.

*

In junior high, beneath a late afternoon
fall of *aurora borealis*, Merry Zumwalt
gathered my heart into a specimen container.
I was in the library, diagramming sentences,
when she and her posse appeared at the window,
their voices lilting through the opaque winter air:

> *Would you like to swing on a star?*
> *And carry Marck Beggs home in a jar?*

I felt, at once, released and trapped,
and I responded with all the grace
and thoughtfulness of a stick.

Clearly, my tender brain concluded, the heart
exists outside of the individual, among alternative
laws of time and space, where any passersby
could simply reach out and poke it
or squeeze it. And so I loaned it out
to all the inarticulate dolts populating the landscape
like spring mold. I became their private Cyrano,
writing love-drenched missives to their beautiful girlfriends
who would never even learn my name.
But they knew my words and would recite them
to each other by their lockers between classes,
my heart passing between them
as easily as handshakes and stolen glances.

*

In college, I started hanging out with my brain
and all of its nefarious friends and influences:
alcohol, Eliot, coffee, bohemians, Kafka, peyote,
Zappa, sugar, politics, and computers.
Somewhere off in the shadows, my heart
stood by and watched as I fumbled through
a maze of women, their names a litany of brilliance, cruelty,
promises, and lies. Through decades of neglect,
my heart never complained, never judged,
as my brain went on terrible rampages,
cutting through relationships like slave labor
in a rain forest, leaving behind burnt ruins
as my poor, sad heart wandered aimlessly to nowhere.

★

Nowhere, it turns out, is a small auditorium
where I sat down in the dark
to escape myself. As you coaxed music,
slowly, from the bowels of the Bösendorfer,
my heart sat straight up and looked at you hard,
as if I suddenly understood that rock
in my garden was a diamond.

My heart came to you a limping mess
of an organ, cheapened by an easy, thoughtless life,
the brain's whore in every sense.
It wasn't the music, nor even your eyes—
when I grasped your hand for the first time,
my heart discovered it was home.
Nowhere, it turns out, is somewhere.

II.

A Cabin in the Woods

History shows that very often violence does work.
  —Theodore John Kaczynski

*I didn't appreciate how good he really was until one day...
I came across a recently arrived journal in the mathematics
library that featured an article written by 'T. J. Kaczynski.' So
while most of us were trying to learn to arrange logical statements
into coherent arguments, Ted was quietly solving open problems
and creating new mathematics. It was as if he could write poetry
while the rest of us were struggling to learn grammar!*
  —Joel Shapiro (fellow grad student)

One world at a time.
  —Henry David Thoreau

*Thoreau went to Walden Pond for earnest, elevated reasons.
He was in search of Life. He was also in search of simple living
conditions that would permit him to concentrate on his writing.*
  —Robert D. Richardson, Jr.
    (intellectual biographer)

Nine Dialogues

Prologues

Theodore John Kaczynski

I am not insane, but that
is a trick of the law
because the insane never admit and, thereby, do.
Harvard, on the other hand,
was a tripwire of insanity: the student
as labrat for Murray
and his witchhunt of freshman souls.
Murray with his verbal breakdown
of the central nervous system, of neurons.
Murray with his breakthrough techniques
of interrogation. The truth but a brilliant splinter
of abstractions: one to suit you,
one to suit him, the rest
a garbage heap of grey matter and pelts.
Behind his mirror, I thought I spied myself,
but then grasped the Ivy League of terror.
There is no code for what I am about
to tell you. Each word is its own symbol.

Henry David Thoreau

The heart of man is a sad metaphor
for God. The woods represent open mind,
sending man on a quest for meaning.
But as the mind opens to so much hope,
does the blood-gorged heart listen to reason?
Choose any man and his reputation:
would it make sense to a goose that a man
guilty of murder should himself be killed?
Would it make sense for a lover to die
inch by inch, day after day, so confined
within the jail of abstract emotion?
You are so clever, perhaps, that you think
the goose, a thousand feet up, does not see
the whole picture. You trust in myopic
visions tainted by an inner mural.
Forgive yourself, if you can, for no god
ever claimed to be created by man,
and yet no true god can claim otherwise.
What I tell you, your mind already knows.

Youth

Ted

If you peel back a label,
it leaves a trail sticky
like snail goop.
Labels hang off you,
broken appendages: *brilliant,*
socially awkward, polite, unresponsive.
You avoid bathing.
You eat less than air,
so as to become invisible.
Your mother will blame all this
on childhood hives and she will lie
her way out of responsibility
when they present you
to the world as unreasonable.
When they show you a monster.

Henry

I was born David Henry, a boy
invisible and turned loose in the world.
It did not see me, but I watched closely:
the river renewing itself again,
trees shedding the past in a flame of leaves.
I thought of the land as my reflection,
and meant for it to see me, my small trace
among its worried stones. I meant to leave
my mark in timeless words, observations
relevant to any men meant to live.
To live. Not to wander as placid sheep
through the civilized world. And so I wrote.
My notebooks brimmed with the turning of light,
with the growth of an oak. Henry David
was born among these journals and set free.

Harvard

Ted

They turned me over, at sixteen,
to the great experimenter.
They turned me into a man
or rat—how was I to know?
They buried me in words
and shut me off in a room

of my own. Do you know how much room
it takes to suffocate? How many words
to break the will of a man?
Here is an experiment:
take everything you imagined as a teen,
subtract from it everything you know.

You will find yourself suddenly known
in a scaldingly bright, mirrored room
discussing the nature of a word
you first learned at sixteen,
the Latin root of experiment,
and the hidden world of a man

watching from behind glass, a man
given to the secret life of this room.
A man beyond the comprehension of a teen,
however clever, beyond what could be known
in the stagnant realm of words.
A man who considers you experimental.

In the middle of this experiment,
he brings in another young man,
whom you believe a friend in this room,
who seems to understand how at sixteen
you feel the need to know
the nature and purpose of words,

but then suddenly turns on your own words
to show how stupid you were at sixteen,
to think you could possibly know
anything that would enlighten this room,
anything that would inform any man
that you are worth the price of this experiment.

The experiment lasts beyond the mirrored room,
beyond your years as a teen, beyond all you have known.
How to become a Harvard man? Fit into a word.

Henry

Would that we had any experiments!
Rote memory, regimentation and
rowdyism were the three R's put forth
under Quincy, the mere school master posing
as scholar. A poor accountant without
a shred of simple curiosity,
he beat down our wills through indifference.
He fed us dry branch when we craved wet root.
Many revolted, but not I, who sat
shivering in my room, warming my feet
on a cannonball, eyeing the fire
lest it die, but also reading outside
Quincy's prescribed vacuum, reading with all
my heart, awaiting Longfellow's next talk,
awaiting the end of this soul numbing,
institutionalized death of the self.
How to become a Harvard man? Don't.

Teaching & Violence

Ted

One poet mocked me as the last man
to wear a suit and tie at Berkeley.
True, perhaps, but what of it?
I quit because how many
atomic bomb-makers do we need?
Ironic, you will think, but only
because you are a fool, a leftist.
What is mathematics to an over-fed,
overly spawning hypocrite like
your average bourgeois college student?
I know who I kill because
I take it personally. I teach everyone
in the splintered aftermath exactly
who is hated and to what degree.
This is how we keep the revolution pure,
by keeping it personal. The great bombs
of society kill many, but without meaning.
Whereas each bomb I send is a textbook,
a love letter to break a single heart.

Henry

Like with religion, I could not remain
in the room, as if the spirit or mind
should be housed in a coffin of windows.
Before I left the schoolhouse, however,
I chose six boys at random, to provide
one last lesson at the end of a cane,
at the end of my wit. And I beat them
as a master beats any slave, without
fear or mercy. Exhausted, I walked out.
I left behind my anger. I left them
a lesson for life: the word made torn flesh.

Love

Ted

Love is how a brother betrays his own,
a mother's storge no less deadly a wound.
A brother's heart is a path of glass stones
while mother's is a poison-filled spoon.

A woman in love with a man is blind
for, in fact, no man can truly be seen.
A man in love eventually finds
in any woman the square root of sin.

Love is a fall into the well of sex,
crudest gratification of the brain.
Love is no language or secret text,
but a grunt delivered in pain…from pain.

Of all the horrors to visit upon man,
love is the razor caressing his hands.

Henry

Ah! But I loved her through my dying breath:
sweet Ellen, my brother, John's, fiancé
until her cold father made her recant.
The only cure for love is but more love,
so I sent her a missive of the heart.
This time her father removed her from view,
yet that sight, even of her neck and back
as I rowed her under the sun, never
has fled the mind's eye. So love is not pain,
but that which separates us from the rest.
Even cynical Voltaire did not mean
for us to confuse the peaks of spirit
with the lowlands of lust. No animals
are we on this earth. No animal could
appreciate that mortal coil of hair
sprung from behind her ear that afternoon.
Truth, order, and beauty bind a man's mind
to his heart, if only he would step back
from the useless toil of his day, to gaze
upon that untouched by his own rough hands.
Even the sensualist, Whitman, knew
this ethereal connection to life.
Even you are not left behind the curve.

Cabins

Ted

Actually, I have two:
one for me, neither for you.

The first I modeled after Thoreau's,
the second is secret, known only to crows.

Miles from nowhere, I test my bombs.
Birdsong from the forest afterward calms.

In a dream, they took my first cabin away
to a shopping mall where children would gaze

on the tiny hovel of a man once removed
from a culture where the individual is never approved.

I lined it with books and small detonators,
gifts to the world, personal favors:

to take the collective mind off liberal angst,
a common threat to rail against.

Two cabins have I, and both have their uses.
Both serve to salve a rash of abuses.

Henry

Man has too much time and money to spare.
Shackled to his father's farm and a house
beyond real needs—what means a man must raise
to keep what he deems important. In time
he enters the vicious cycle of greed,
a slave to his wants, his needs illusory.
I have no need for such a man. A muskrat
makes a better neighbor, and gives no cause
to covet, argue, or even to hate.
If man would feed upon delicious light
of evening fall, he would know the beauty
of the most humble abode, built with sweat,
honest and earned. Enough for any man.

Prison/Jail

Ted

My bed and table
are made of molded concrete.
Each day, I exercise
in a kennel and eye
the sun for an hour.
I write letters informing
my idiot mother not to send
magazines, not to send salted nuts.
I write 20-page answers to psychotherapists
who hand them to their wives
to open. I defend my integrity
against the bullshit modern imagination
which claims to know me.
Would they interpret this cell,
built by taxes in their honor,
in their image, the same as they did
my cabin? For if the cabin
is a manifestation of my mind,
then this cell speaks volumes
about our molded society.
SuperMax? This is the language of those
who should be housed in one.

Henry

I spent a night in jail for refusing
to pay a tax unrepresentative
of me, who would own no man. Margaret
led us up to "the narrow, thorny path
where Integrity leads," and I walked.

The Art of Writing

Ted

I have studied

Words, symbols, and codes.
I am no stranger to whatever power
Language holds over mankind.
Latin, Greek, German, Spanish—

Knowledge is the only key worth possessing.
I would gladly give up the weak virtues:
Love, kindness, altruism.
Lies such as these bring us to superstition, to fiction.

You believe you know better,
Only you cannot see your own way
Unless there is a mirror to guide you.

Henry

Literature can exist in a slip
of paper meant only to list the cost
of constructing a cabin or planting
a plot of beans. Emerson taught us how
to look, to listen—so why should the wind
itself not bring us great words from beyond
the narrow education of our ears?
There is as much Shakespeare in the chuckle
of a squirrel as any book, only
you must listen for it. You must be still.
The classics have much to offer, of course;
we should no sooner neglect rhetoric
than our daily consumption of water.
But nor should we hold aloft any book
over the bowed, sweating back of a man
growing the food to nourish us to read.

Found Poems

Ted (from Industrial Society and Its Future)

Human beings have a need:
the hypothetical case of a man
whether he admits to himself
or not. The Industrial Revolution
should think twice before encouraging
psychological conflict—you can't
eat your cake and have it too.
Science is going to fix all that.
The system to date has been impressively
successful taking knives and guns
away from computer nerds and liberals.
Imagine a society, as we explained,
since the beginning of civilization.
If anyone still imagines
a functioning part of society, it may seem
senseless and well socialized to prove
university professors are as strong and capable
as heterosexual white males,
desperately anxious to prove that women
fell into disrepair and were never rebuilt.
Suppose a biological trait is discovered
for a few passive, inward looking groups,
such as the Amish or the gypsies.
Their loyalties are such that
insatiable depression may be argued, or
that most revolutions have two failures:
Nature and God. By community,
almost impossible for most individuals
and small groups, we mean that
we've had to permanently reduce some human beings.
If you think that big government

interferes in your life too much,
we are reasonably confident
that the best diagnostic trait
to stop widespread life-expectancy
is to eat your cake and kill some people.

Henry   (from Walden)

I went to the woods to walk out the gate
empty-handed without anxiety,
without cowhide boots which I claimed by rights.
I thus found that the student who wished
to build me a house is an illusion.
He has a great bundle of white-oak bark,
he was a great consumer of meat, and
he offered me a drink. How thick the pigeons!
There is a period in the history
of the individual we cannot
but pity—this was my answer. Thus far
I am of the opinion of Chaucer's
nun: there are a clean race of frogs and pouts.
I wanted to suck out all the marrow
of life, to cut a broad swath, to drive life
into a corner whether it is of
the devil or of God. I borrowed an axe,
but it is a characteristic
of wisdom not to do desperate things.

Seven Dreams of
Thoreau & the Unabomber

I.

Thoreau and the Unabomber
sit at a small, dusty table
in a cabin, arm-wrestling
over who is smarter, who
will leave the more lasting impression.

One cannot help but notice
the freckles of dust
riding the sunlight through
the tiny window. One cannot
help but wish a maid would enter.

II.

Thoreau and the Unabomber
stand in front of an ATM,
arguing about who has less money,
fewer material attachments.

"For over two decades," argues Ted,
"I have lived off less than four hundred dollars
a year! I nearly starved more than once!"

"Ah! See how married you are to money
and its greedy pursuit," argues Henry.
"You should have just borrowed more stuff.
You should have walked home for a chicken dinner
and a load of laundry once in a while."

III.

Thoreau and the Unabomber
are in an Irish pub, staring
at a plump, redheaded woman
throwing darts. "If she were mine,"
swoons Henry, "I would show her
the star-eaten blanket of the night,
and bathe in the cool stream of her eyes."

"If she were yours," answers Ted,
"I would mail you a gift."

IV.

Thoreau and the Unabomber
are poking Buddha's belly,
laughing uproariously like schoolboys.

Buddha sighs and suggests
they might find better use
of their time. "What would you suggest?" asks Henry.

Buddha closes his eyes to consider an answer.
Upon opening them, he sees a cabin
at the high end of a kite string.

V.

Thoreau and the Unabomber
visit my cabin in Arkansas.
Wide-eyed and nearly speechless,
startled by its spaciousness.

"Why, you could fit both our cabins,
along with Ted's secret one, in here
and still have room to dance!" exclaims Henry.

"I don't really want to dream
about you dancing," I respond.

"Well, let's get this over with,"
says Ted, as he snatches up
Henry's hands and twirls him.

"Oh!" I gasp.

"I was in the woods for twenty-two years,"
says Ted. " Surely you do not think
I thought of nothing but bombs."

VI.

Thoreau and the Unabomber
are hiking a rocky trail
deep into the Sangre de Cristo Mountains.
It is a difficult walk for Henry
because of the altitude and because
he is used to the calm, manicured trails
of New England. Ted thinks Henry
a bit of a fancy pants. However,
at the lower Lake of the Clouds,
Henry catches a trout for lunch,
using only a safety pin and
a ball of twine. Ted has not enjoyed food
for a long time so much as he drools
over this little fish. He looks up
to see an eagle intersect the path
of an airplane and wonders
if any of his students at Berkeley are dead.

VII.

Thoreau and the Unabomber
arrive at Bloomsburywest,
a writer's retreat in Colorado,
and Ted immediately rifles
through the books. "Clearly,"
he declares, "the proprietress
is a leftist of some sort.
Most likely a feminist."

"But Ted," says Henry. "Look!
String cheese and green salsa…
and no television."

"Kind of feminine, though, wouldn't
you agree?" asks Ted.
"All these bright colors,
all this art."

"Actually," answers Henry, while
claiming the top bunk to better keep
and eye on Ted in the night,
"Matisse was a man, and
women do not own particular hues."

But Ted is no longer listening
as he spies the shack in the backyard.
"A secret cabin," he thinks to himself,
"a room of my own, indeed."